Enlighten Your Life

The Six Principles

By Jeffery Beach
Beach Books

© Copyright 2007 Jeffery Beach

Table of Contents

Acknowledgments xix

Introduction 3

Chapter 1 25

Chapter 2 29

Chapter 3 33

Chapter 4 37

Chapter 5 47

Chapter 6 49

Chapter 7 55

Chapter 8 63

Chapter 9 67

Chapter 10 69

Chapter 11 77

Conclusion 81

Dedicated to Matt George

He Found His Path

Namaste: "I salute the Divine in you."

"May all mother sentient beings
Boundless as the sky,
Have happiness and the causes of happiness.
May they be liberated from suffering and the
causes of suffering.
May they never be separated from the happiness,
Which is free from sorrow.
May they rest in equanimity,
Free from attachment and aversion."

Tibetan prayer called, "Altruistic Motivation"

Acknowledgments

I have had the great good fortune to enjoy meeting and learning from many good teachers in my life, starting with my parents who gave me a value system of respect for others. There were men and women from all arenas whose words propelled me to walk my walk. Whether it was a few profound words or an extended interaction with them, I want to take this time to thank and acknowledge each and every one of them. I also want to thank those teachers yet to come.

Introduction

Before you read any further, and whenever you pick up this book, take a few minutes to relax your body, your speech, and your mind.

How? One of the simplest ways used by enlightened men and women for thousands of years is as follows:

Sit on the edge of a chair or a cushion. Put your hands on your knees or folded in your lap. Curl the tip of your tongue upward, lightly touching the front part of the roof of your mouth. Breathe gently into the lower part of your abdomen and relax…. Imagine Infinite Boundless Light entering your body, filling a golden bowl, four fingers below your navel.

Relax. Let go of all that you love, all your aversions, and all your hopes and fears.

Imagine that all your thoughts are like clouds in the sky, sometimes obscuring the sun, but never remaining constant.

Watch your thoughts float by and '**Just Be**'. Be in the present moment. Be in the moment of your breath. Meditate in this way every day for thirty minutes or more. If you can't do it for that long, work up to it. Start with five minutes, and slowly add more time as it feels comfortable for you to do.

Once, a disciple asked his teacher how he could repay him for the knowledge and wisdom he had received. The teacher replied, "You must practice and empower others to practice." You, too, can do this; because you can, you must teach others how to empower themselves with this meditation. If this chain of practice and empowerment continues uninterrupted, imagine the effect on the world!

Generosity begins with sharing. This is true generosity, and through generosity comes the unfolding of your Wisdom Heart. Opening your Wisdom Heart is just a name for the personal process you have within yourself to let go of all your sufferings, which are, in essence, your attachments and aversions. It's about beginning to live to your fullest potential. The power of your potential resides in the underlying primordial energy of All That Is. To surrender to a state of no power, you open yourself to the only power: the Primordial Spirit. The Primordial Spirit is that which encompasses all things. It is not separate. It's infinite and therefore cannot be defined by finite words or language:

> *The Tao that can be named*
> *Is not the eternal Tao.*
> *The God that can be named*
> *Is not God.*
> *Enlightenment that is named*
> *Is not Enlightenment.*
> *The Buddha that can be named*
> *Is not the Buddha.*

The 'essence' that is the Primordial Spirit makes it impossible for anything outside of itself to exist. What you can realize, within you, is the experience of being this Primordial Spirit. It is, in essence, the underlying, unifying principle of 'All That Is'. Meditate in the present moment and you will experience it. Be in this present moment. Feel it, don't define it. In the present moment, there is no defining of anything.

In our lives, we have spiritual moments every day. Whether it is something major like a near-death experience, or something smaller, like looking up at the stars at night and feeling a connection with the cosmos that reaches in all directions.

Tuning our awareness into these things is tuning into the Primordial Spirit. Meditation is a good way to get in touch with it. Meditation opens us up to the 'small still voice' inside that guides all those who stop long enough to hear it. Listening to that 'small still voice' within begins the development of faith in our connection to all things and the connection of all things to us.

Nothing can exist of and by itself. All things come into being interdependently and originate from their causes. In turn, these things become the cause of new effects.

Self-confidence takes root in the act of letting go of attachments to minor agitations, to obstacles, fears, desires, and hopes. These attachments hold you back from accomplishing meaningful goals in your life. You can let go because that 'still voice' inside will never fail to guide you. The more you let go, the more you will have 'self-mastery', and with 'self-mastery', you will become fearless. As you travel on the path of your individual search for wisdom and compassion, the strength of this search is reinforced by this act of faith.

There is a danger of over-intellectualizing the unfolding process of wisdom. Don't analyze or speculate on it too much. Embracing this belief gives one an experiential understanding of how expanded consciousness leads to a richer and more fulfilling life; the more faith in this process you develop, the less you will speculate on and analyze your progress. "In a God-created universe, the secret of life is no power. When we come to a place of no power, then no power can operate against us, in us, or through us. That puts us in a very humble position where much as we dislike doing it, we have to acknowledge as Jesus did, 'I can, of mine own self, do nothing.' That's the goal of this message: to come to a place where we won't pay lip service to the statement, 'I can of mine own self do nothing,' but where we can demonstrate that it's actually true and let whatever it is that's the power of God, the no-power, assert itself and do the work."[1]

This very moment, this 'Present Moment,' is the 'State of Suchness' that sages from all ages allude to as the enlightened state. Unfortunately, instead of **Being: Now**, we let our minds wander through the

---

[1] Joel Goldsmith 'The Thunder of Silence' Harper & Brothers, Publishers, New York 1961

vast ocean of duality that is the physical world and handicap ourselves with the burden of self-cherishing. We let our minds wander in the past; we let it wander in the future. **To Be: Now**, is the state of emptiness, of suchness, and it is the only way to tap into the eternal quality of the Primordial Essence of all things and find the effortless clarity of mindfulness. "All phenomena revert to stillness. Truly inconceivable is this truth."[2]

This Primordial Essence is not something different from the Tao or God. In truth, since they are infinite, how can there be anything else? All things are just the expression of the Infinite. This is why Buddhists meditate on the union of appearance and emptiness. Try it some time. Sit quietly, breathe into the lower part of your abdomen, and relax. "Breath is one's own mind; one's own mind does the breathing. Once the mind stirs, then there is energy. Energy is basically an emanation of mind."[3] Let your thoughts

---

[2] 'Secret of the Golden Flower' Translated by Thomas Cleary, Harper One Publishers 1993

[3] 'Secret of the Golden Flower' Translated by Thomas Cleary, Harper One Publishers 1993

flow naturally. They can do no harm. Thoughts have no power. There is nothing to fear. Now, view your thoughts as only moments in time, as impermanent as clouds. Realize too that all material things are just as impermanent. Nothing stays the same forever.

> *"All things are like dreams, illusions,*
> *Bubbles, shadows…*
> *Like dew drops and a lightning flash,*
> *Contemplate them thus."*[4]

Being: Now, means that in the exact moment of the present, you are no longer thinking of the past, you are no longer thinking of the future. In the present moment, you can't have conceptual thoughts, because you can't think when you are in the Now. You just are. Furthermore, everything else just is. This is the relinquishment of self-cherishing and the beginning of the development of a compassionate mind. This is the state of Grace,

---

[4] The Diamond Sutra of Mahayana Buddhism

referred to in Christian texts, in which you receive the essence of Primordial Energy.

Meditation, done every day, will improve your health and your mental acuity. If you aren't used to meditating, you might find it difficult to sit for thirty minutes. However, if you start with five minutes and gradually increase your meditation time, you will find thirty minutes easy to do. If you can do more, that is even better. Don't doubt yourself, this something anyone can accomplish. Take one step at a time. You always make great spiritual progress in this fashion and can help others along the way by sharing your growth and understanding.

What I share in this book is not new. The Six Principles expressed in this book are nothing more than the Six Perfections of Buddhism, otherwise known as the Six Paramitas. I wrote this book for those who may not have an interest in religion yet find themselves drawn to the universal principles that lie within. Universal principles transcend any particular religion or philosophy and can be written in a language acceptable to anyone. Many people have taught these words before me. Nevertheless, they bear repeating. The message is timeless and repeating it here, increases retention of its content, so that it is remembered, and, more importantly, not forgotten. Mostly, I wrote this book to remind myself to practice what I preach.

Now, let go.... Let go of all attachments and cravings. Let go of your aversions. They are but an expression of self-cherishing and self-cherishing is the expression of the fundamental ignorance that repeatedly binds humanity to make the same mistakes.

Remember that there are always people who are worse off than you. Therefore, let go of your fears, your aversions, and your attachments. Let go of the things that truly hold you back. There is no reason for fearing letting go. Fear is a mental formation of your own making. Admiral Halsey once said, "There are no great men, only great challenges that ordinary men rise up to meet." The aversions we have for things in this world are no different from our attachments. Attachments and aversions are the hopes and fears brought on by the self-cherishing that holds us back from doing the things that might truly benefit us. We must realize that the essence of this universe is its transitory, unfolding nature in which all things are born, live and die. Enjoy life as it is, for all it is, the good and the bad, because, in truth, there is no good and no evil. Good and evil are only mental fabrications and in this way, we must treat everyone with respect, because we don't know who that person may be. There is an old Tibetan saying,

> *"There reason I am not free from suffering,*
> *Is that I have only been caring for myself*
> *From beginningless time.*
> *Now, I should practice caring*
> *Only about others.*
> *This is the source of virtue and happiness."*[5]

---

[5] Jigme Tenpe Nyima

If you believe in reincarnation (if you don't believe in reincarnation, think of it as a metaphor or analogy for the different periods of your life), we must remember that all sentient beings, from beginningless time, in one life or another, have been your mother. Treating all sentient beings as if they were our mothers is a good first step towards living compassionately and lovingly. Living in a state of love and compassion towards all beings develops the inborn primordial wisdom innate in all of us. Living in the spirit of love and compassion allows miracles to happen. We can truly allow these miracles to happen while enlightening our lives.

As the story goes, a number of years ago, Mother Theresa went to war-ravaged Beirut, Lebanon to rescue the children of an orphanage stuck in the middle of a terrible battle. When she arrived in the city, there was, naturally, great concern for her safety and many begged her not to go to the orphanage. Mother Theresa would not be deterred. She told all concerned that she would go to the orphanage the very next day. She then retired for the evening. In the morning, for some unexplained reason, the fighting stopped completely. Mother Theresa and her entourage went to the orphanage and brought all the children to safety. Shortly afterward, the fighting began again. To me, the lull in the fighting was Mother Theresa's great compassion and the power of her prayers of love. Going to an orphanage in the middle of a battleground was not an act of foolhardiness on her part. It was an act of emptying herself of any notion of 'I and Thou.' It was an act of surrender to that place of no personal power and letting the energy of God, the Primordial Spirit take over and express itself in grace and faith in Mother Theresa.

Compassionate acts overcome any obstacle, any fear. Compassionate living is the path to wisdom. It is the foundation for conviction and faith in the power of life and love.

Take charge of your life. Be responsible for it because no one else will. Take charge of your life because today may be your last day. Your life is very precious. Make sure what you do is a product of your conclusions, of your awakenings. You can't go back in time to correct your mistakes. You can go forward and not repeat them.

Don't be a follower, be a student. A real student assimilates what he's learned from his teachers, he doesn't imitate them. Be yourself, and through being yourself express the truths you learned.

It is easy to be lazy of spirit, but life is short; before we know it, it is over. One way to overcome the laziness of spirit is not to bite off more than we can chew. However, we can't make this an excuse for doing too little. The way to climb a mountain is one step at a time. A journey of a thousand miles begins with the first step. Take the first step toward the light in your life. Then, take one more, then one more, and one more, until this journey becomes like second nature to you. We mustn't punish ourselves, but we must not lightly excuse ourselves either. To be born as a human being is a very precious gift and each moment of 'now', is a 'present'. We might admire other forms of life such as a soaring bird and fantasize what it would be like to be reborn as such an animal. However, we will never be able to accomplish in that form what we can as human beings. Because of the difficulties, we face in life, and this includes our constant striving for happiness, we forget the opportunities to practice our spirituality as the most exalted purpose for living.

Understand life's changes.

You can't alter the fact that everyone faces difficulties, but we can change our view of them. All things in this world are impermanent. We can learn to handle the winters. The winters of life always come, but so do the springs, the summers, and the falls. We can get wiser, stronger, and better by accepting the impermanent nature of all things. Mentally, we will grow. A mind once thus expanded, can then return to its state of openness and awareness. We mustn't settle for what we are. We must settle for what we can be. Strive for excellence and develop more patience. We can make compassion for all life the focus of our lives. Compassion is the ultimate form of patience. We should be especially patient towards those we don't like, fear, or don't know. It is easy to be compassionate towards the ones we love, but true compassion expresses itself towards all beings regardless of who they are, just like the sun, the moon, and the stars shine on all without prejudice. Sharing and giving are an integral part of refining the spirit.

From compassion, wisdom arises. Study, practice, and meditate. Respect everybody, for you don't know to whom you may be talking. Cynicism closes the possibilities and channels of life. It shrivels the soul. Compassion manifests in infinite ways and manifesting it through ourselves, we will develop in infinite ways. Therefore, it makes sense to be kind and accepting.

Good things happen. Bad things happen. Sometimes out of good, there is an ensuing bad outcome, and sometimes out of bad, there is an ensuing good outcome. The importance we attach to circumstances gives them power over our lives and takes power from us. By giving power to an event, we give it a reality and subordinate ourselves to it by attachment or aversion. Our thought patterns sway to this beat out of habit. However, events cannot exist of and by themselves. Conceptual existence of any kind can't be without its supporting interdependent components of causes and conditions. Therefore, the mind gives power to circumstances.

All of us achieve some experiential understanding of different relative qualities in the events of our lives. Without this understanding, we couldn't function in any commanding fashion and we would be no different than a falling leaf blown about by a puff of wind. For example, it's this type of understanding that gives children the confidence and conviction to begin walking and talking. This relative experiential understanding, however, doesn't give us insight into the absolute nature of reality, into the impermanence of all things. It doesn't promote spiritual fearlessness and confidence while walking on the path from birth to death. What promotes truly rooted self-confidence in all things, spiritual and mundane, is the realization that the interdependently arising impermanent nature of all causes and conditions forming material reality, is the continuum of all existence.

The Six Principles are about integrating enlightened living into daily life, carrying their circumstances into our personal path, and assimilating them into our awakening to the light of conscious living.

Chapter 1

The First Training

The Six Principles divide into three pieces of training: ethical behavior, meditation, and wisdom. The first training is the path of virtue, ethics, integrity, self-discipline, and excellence. This training cools the heat of our passions and emotions. It's like a shade in the desert of our conflicting emotions, a shelter where we can find relief. Non-attachment, integrity, and a righteous, honest life provide shelter, cooling shade in these confusing times. To have virtue means not harming. It means having integrity and honesty. We all have that capacity in our core, we only need to open to this place in ourselves. We all have this innate gift, even if we don't reveal it very often. We have the faculty, to be honest, and virtuous, not self-righteous, or do things for the rewards we might well believe will be the result of our actions. To live by example, by living a righteous life, free from self-cherishing is enlightened living and by that inference, an enlightened life. Enlightenment's essential quality is completely dependent on the way we live our lives.

We can train externally by exercising restraint from harming others, or ourselves, in any way. We can work from the inside out, from our innate goodness and integrity, by meditating and resting in the actual moment of the present without clinging to anything, free from concepts, attachments, and aversions, resulting in our natural integrity, and our natural integrity flowing without complications or restrictions. This is the way to give up self-cherishing and embrace the cherishing of others instead.

The best way to train from the outside in and from the inside out at the same time. Then wherever we are, it can flower, and our highest character will arise.

Enlightened living is living impeccably. It is not rules or vows, it is not rigid integrity, but it is the practice of impeccable behavior, character, and integrity. When we change for the better, our children, our grandchildren, and the world will change for the better. I find it interesting that people of high character, by default, become the natural leaders, in some fashion or another, in the world. In life there are those of true high character in all social strata, some are well known some are not, whose light shines forth. We can't help but look up to them and guide ourselves by their example.

Chapter 2

The Second Training

The second training is in developing collectedness, concentration, reflection, inquiry, mindfulness, meditation, and focus. From this, we develop discernment, energy, joy, lightness, recollection, concentration, and non-attachment to our involvement in the events of daily life. This training will transform the foundation of our consciousness from relying on the afflictions of attachment and aversion, an openness of mind, no longer leaning on the mind's conceptual fabrications as objective reality. We become tranquil.

"There is one kind of tranquility, and there are also four because there is one kind of tranquility in each of the four immeasurables: immeasurable kindness, immeasurable compassion, immeasurable joy, and immeasurable equanimity."[6]

The second training of enlightened living is meditation. Meditation internalizes our understanding. Then, our understanding becomes experiential in nature. We will know what we speak. The experiential approach of meditation sharpens intellectual comprehension. Just like eating a pear gives a knowing of its taste that description can't provide.

Spiritual conviction gives us the power to control the relationship we have with the experience of living. This is the true meaning of freedom. We can develop conviction by meditation. The result of meditation is a knowing, conviction, commitment, and faith arising without effort. It is in centering in the present. This is real power. It is this power that enables us to manage the circumstances of our lives with confidence and fearlessness.

---

[6] Sandhinirmochanasutra 'Scripture Unlocking the Mysteries', a complete sourcebook of Buddhist yoga, a comprehensive course. Translated by Thomas Cleary. Shambala Publications, Inc. 1995

To some, meditation and mindfulness, including explicit forms of religious or philosophical self-inquiry, look like they are without merit. Yet, without this internal component, we would have no depth; we would only be going through the motions, performing empty rituals and giving mere lip service to the high ideals of enlightened living. Are we interested in this work? Are we inquiring? Are we applying ourselves and investigating? What is our motivation? Are we only sitting down and trying to stop ourselves from thinking? Pills do that. That is not the point of meditation. The point of meditation is to improve the quality of investigating, or inquiring, of being more aware and conscious, and that is the difference. It is an experiential difference. Awareness is part of all of us. We all have a pure, authentic spiritual presence. It's our inner light, our 'in-light', and our stillness within. Consciousness is what illuminates us. It is inherently present. It is always here and now. We are totally here, in every moment, even if we feel scattered, we are lit by presence, by innate awareness: it is the light within us all. Finding the light or enlightened within, is in your DNA, your body, mind, and spirit, it is your birth, right here and now. This leads to the third training.

Chapter 3

The Third Training

The third training is the development of wisdom, knowing, enlightened awareness, transcendent wisdom, and true self-knowledge. The third training is really no more than an internalization and practice of the first two pieces of training. The third training of enlightened living is wisdom. Wisdom is hard to describe, and yet, it is so palpable. We can feel it outwardly functioning in life, very practically, as wisdom, common sense, or genuine selfless helpfulness. Usually, wise people are wise about life and its continuous opportunities to become aware. They are wise in the ways of the world: wise in life and wise about death. To others, it shows up as wisdom, being wise, being an elder, mentor, or a role model. We too can develop that. It may seem too subtle to perceive, however when we look at ourselves, it is still there. We can cultivate it as sanity, and centeredness. We can be at home with both others and ourselves. This way we can investigate the deep inner source of our being and heal. Knowing, transcendence, and unselfishness is within us all. The ultimate form of wisdom is not a doing; it is our true nature, our being. It is not only information or intellectual knowledge. Even though wisdom sounds like knowledge, in reality, it is our pure, luminous being, going far beyond the ordinary perceptions of life. Can we focus on this? Yes! It is not just a doing, not just a knowing, but can we be it? Yes! Can we trust it? It is the only thing we can fully trust.

Being is complete in itself. That is the nature of transcendental wisdom. Our being is a mystical sacrament, it is the mysterious and sacred grace of the present moment. It has been around a lot longer than churches or religions. It is not our personal being but being itself. It is in all living things.

Virtue, meditation or awareness practice and wisdom make up the three conscious methods upon which enlightened living can rest. The three are inseparable, each supporting and promoting the other. For example, if we lie, steal, or have weak moral fiber, how can we think to know the truth?

Chapter 4

Generosity

The Six Principles are the natural practices of life and living. In some way, we can say that the sixth principle, experiential wisdom, is the philosophy or the view of an enlightened being, and the other five principles, such as generosity, integrity, patience, diligence, and meditation are the conducting or the practice of enlightened life.

The first principle of enlightened life is the integration of generosity of spirit and action in all that we do. Christians call this charity. The word comes from the Latin word 'Caritas', which means unconditional caring; it doesn't only mean giving pennies to the poor. 'Caritas' means unattached generosity, boundless openness, and unconditional love: **Open Heart, Open Mind, Open Hand.**

A closed fist holds nothing.
An open hand holds the world.

It is wise to let go of our attachments and aversions. Resistance to letting go is suffering. Cravings and attachments are suffering. Aversions are suffering. It is wise to let them go. Outwardly, this implies becoming more generous, open, giving, serving, and donating our time and energy. Internally, it is becoming more generous with our emotions, being openhearted, not suppressing our emotions not being miserly with them rather, allowing them to be, and appreciating them. It is being generous, spontaneous, and with total unbounded energy. Why squelch that limitless, innate energy like a miser, as if saving you energy for the 'real thing'? Many people suffer by holding back and fearing intimate engagement and total involvement. We can miss our whole life that way. Just being is innate generosity. Everything is available to us within the natural state of being. Let's not be miserly in being and by that miserliness we, then, are lost in doing and squandering our energies in frivolous, scattered activities. All things are available in the natural state of pure being.

There are three major categories of generosity. With the first category, there is the giving of wealth and there is both inner and outer wealth. Outer wealth and its symbols, we all understand. Inner wealth refers to one's own head, brain, eyes, and words. For those poor and disabled, we help them with money and goods for living. If people cannot survive, aren't satisfied with their basic needs, they will not listen to what you say and follow what you do. Though the help is sometimes minimal, it is an immediate solution to relieve them from suffering, starving, coldness, and so on. With the immeasurable mind of compassion, a conscious person doesn't hesitate to help under these circumstances.

Generosity should be practiced first toward oneself. In doing so, we should charge our minds and bodies with positive thoughts of peace and happiness. We should think about how to be peaceful, happy, and free from suffering, worry, and anger. We then become the embodiment of generosity. Shielded by loving-kindness, we cut off hostile vibrations and negative thoughts. We become ever tolerant and try our best not to give in to anger towards anyone. When we are full of peace and happiness and free from thoughts of anger and other negativities, it is easy to radiate loving-kindness. Before we try to make others happy, we should first be happy ourselves. Then we radiate loving-kindness to those near and dear to us, individually and collectively. After that, we radiate our loving-kindness towards those to whom we have no feelings, wishing for them the same happiness as we wish for ourselves. Finally, we radiate our loving-kindness towards those who are inimical to us. This is difficult but achievable.

The second category, teaching, benefits others, enabling them to improve their performance, and thereby help others as well. To teach someone to fish is better than giving him a fish. We have to teach those who have no skills for work, to give them the ability to work in society, to earn a living without relying on the financial support of others. This is the means to end material poverty. Financial resources are unlimited. Yet, money is not the ultimate solution to all problems. Fundamentally, we have to help others improve their circumstances that led them to where they are now.

There is a fearless quality to giving. We have to help those who live in vexation, fear, and despair and encourage them to overcome any difficulties they encounter. The third category of generosity is the giving of fearlessness. If someone encounters a frightening experience and you comfort them and deliver them from distress and terror, you have made a gift of fearlessness. The Buddha said, "***Giving transforms those who are stingy. Greedy people who don't know how to give should practice giving, for if they don't learn to give, they will never get rid of their stinginess.***"

An enlightened life means living with a sense of natural generosity. We need not look for a worthy purpose to our giving. It is our obligation to give. A conscious person is always ready to render, willingly and humbly, every possible aid. A conscious person isn't concerned as to whether the recipient truly thanks or appreciates the help because there is no expectation of any reward. Moreover, a conscious person makes no distinction between one being or another in giving and is interested only in the good act.

The practice of giving is a vast and comprehensive practice. True giving permeates all aspects of personal and social life. It is the core practice for transforming our ordinary existence and living to the fullest. Getting into the habit of giving and sharing with others is the seed of loving-kindness towards all beings. It is not an easy practice, but with persistence, we can internalize it, and notice how rewarding loving kindness is. This foundation of generosity begins with three concepts.

Non-desire

Non-desire is in the gradual giving up of our cravings and aversions to things and emotions because we continually begin to see their temporary, unfulfilling nature. Our self-cherishing begins to dissipate and true freedom is born with the fearlessness of spirit becoming its expression.

Non-hate

Hatred is another aspect of craving and aversion. Denial of that which we crave makes us frustrated. If these denials continue for a long time, bitterness and anger take root. Letting go of cravings shakes loose the grip this has on our lives and with that comes more equanimity. Awareness of others' suffering arises. Then generosity can take hold.

Non-cruelty

Non-cruelty means to do no harm to others.

Generosity is first among the Six Principles of an awakened life and in its practice, we engender all Six Principles. It is extraordinarily pertinent to our daily life and path. It is the wind in the sails of our transformation from ordinary life to the sunrise of enlightened living.

Chapter 5

Living with Integrity

The second principle is virtue, ethics, or integrity. It is wise not to harm. This is the essence of virtue. It is the essence of ethics. It is the essence of integrity. There should be no self-deception on this matter. It is better to build integrity and develop character. Fundamentally, we all have a purity of heart and basic goodness, and we feel love naturally. It is just a matter of letting it surface and shine. Let's not lose touch with it. Let's enjoy this innate natural resource, rather than exploit others for what we think we need and want. Rather than self-cherishing, let's exploit our own natural resource within, our own true essence of loving kindness and compassion. This essence is something we can never lose; no one and nothing can take that away from us. When we give up self-cherishing and focus on cherishing all beings with impartiality and without exception, we will have no enemies, we will have no fear. When we have no fear, there is nothing we can't do. True compassion manifests in the cherishing of others.

> *"If you try to kill all of your enemies,*
> *You will never succeed.*
> *If you kill your anger,*
> *You will have no enemies."*[7]

---

[7] Shantideva, an Indian Buddhist master who wrote "The Bodhisattva's Way of Life." The are many editions of this work available in print.

Chapter 6

Being in Patience

The third principle of an awakened life is patience, tolerance, forbearance, and acceptance of people and other beings. It's counting to ten and taking a deep breath before we react to a situation. It's having some balance and a sense of restraint. It's patience instead of irritability and anger. It means persevering through whatever twists and turns our path requires to reach the goals of our aspirations. It means being patient, having acceptance and tolerance for people and situations. Endurance and patience mean to be able to bear insult or distress without resentment. It's having patience with everyone's, as well as our foibles, hang-ups, and neuroses. Practicing patience and tolerance, instead of seeing the ugliness in others, we try to seek the good and the beautiful in all.

Don't try to be too perfect and boring. It's good to be a little nuts. It lets the light through and shakes our tree like the wind. Perfection will only frustrate us anyway. Having rocks in a stream makes it sing. Obstacles are steppingstones when we open to their potential. Since we're in this ever-changing mysterious life, we should, therefore, be interested in seeing it through to the end, with openness. We aren't going anywhere else, this is it! That is why, as people get older, they become wiser. They realize that no matter what they do they will pass on. Today, I was watching a young woman crossing the street, moving away from me. She was the portrait of youthful beauty and sexiness. Also crossing the street coming towards me was an old man, struggling with the weakness of age, no longer could he be seen as sexy and attractive. Now, in my life, I am somewhere in between the two, closer to the old man and rapidly moving away from any semblance of youthful beauty and vigor. Sooner than later, I will be like that old man and then I will pass on. There is nothing I can do about it. In fact, I could die at any time, at any moment. Accepting this, I can move towards wisdom. Accepting this, I can view others marching towards old age, sickness, and death. Accepting that, I can understand that all things, all conditions, all concepts, are also born, get old, decay, and die. Accepting, I become patient and allow for the unfolding of events to take place as they will and without judgment. This is the secret, mystical meaning of forbearance, and it will lead us to wisdom. No matter what, all of us are in it for the whole journey. We mustn't be deceived by mere appearances. "This too shall pass," literally means that all things and situations are impermanent; taking this to heart leads to patient behavior. There is nothing permanent in this life. All moments, good and bad, have a beginning and an end. Patience is a priceless gem, which few know how to mine, but if we master it, everything will work out. Patience transforms those who are hateful. If you have an unreasonable temper, cultivate patience and forbearing. Don't be the person who is angry all day and not on speaking terms with anyone unless it is to speak while glaring with angry eyes. Be patient instead. Patience means to bear insults. It means to take what we can't take. For example, if someone hits or scolds us, and we don't retaliate in any way, we have patience. If someone hits us and we hit right back, we can't call that patience; but if someone hits us in the face and we turn the other cheek, we are practicing patience. Not striking back is having patience. Patience is the doctrine of non-violence taken to the degree that it encompasses any situation.

"Though robbers should sever your limbs with a two-handled saw, yet if you thereby defile your mind, you would be no follower of my teaching. Thus, you should train yourselves: Unsullied shall our hearts remain. No evil shall escape our lips. Kind and compassionate with loving-heart, harboring no ill-will shall we abide, enfolding even these bandits with thoughts of loving-kindness. And forth from them proceeding, we shall abide radiating the whole world with thoughts of loving-kindness, vast, expansive, measureless, benevolent, and unified."[8]

Looking at positives instead of the negatives is an easy way to be patient.

---
[8] The Buddha's speech in the Kakacupama Sutta

Chapter 7

Living Enthusiastically

Patience ties directly into the fourth principle of enlightened living: energy, diligence, courage, enthusiasm, or effort. Effort refers here to mental strength rather than physical strength. It is defined as persistent effort in working for the benefit of others, in thought and action. Firmly establishing us in this enlightened principle, we develop self-reliance and make it one of the most prominent behavioral characteristics of our natures.

Enlightened living means one works for others ceaselessly and untiringly, expecting no reward in return.

A conscious person is always ready to serve others to the best of his or her ability. This is the true definition of courage.

Enlightened living regards failure as the step to success, danger as the trigger for courage, and affliction as the key to wisdom. This is the true meaning of enthusiasm.

Enlightened living means never considering a wholesome matter too insignificant or an unwholesome one too small. It is often an effort to leave dull, ordinary thoughts, and it is much for the average person to have fear rather than faith. Faith is an effort of will. This is the meaning of effort. At first, it is an effort; the effort becomes energy, and energy becomes the passion of our true vocation: what we do day and night out of love for all beings. It's not the effort of getting through our work week and forgetting about it on the weekend. That may seem like an effort. However, it's the internal effortless effort and passion for our genuine life that is real. Aren't we all interested in our well-being? Doesn't that make an effort worthwhile to pursue? Aren't we pursuing it day in and day out? It is the courage and fearlessness to pursue our highest good continuously. Inherently, of course, there is boundless energy, interest, curiosity, wonder, beauty, and awe in everything, every moment, and if we open to it, if we don't close ourselves off from it if we don't dull ourselves by immersing into our self-cherishing, we will see the infinite in and from which we can solve our problems. Inexhaustible resources and potential are always available to us in finding everything we seek. It's always in the present moment, in pure being, endless being, and an inexhaustible field of being, inseparable and undifferentiated from all things.

We can make great efforts to improve ourselves, to learn, to grow, and develop: to relinquish what is negative and adopt what is wholesome and positive, but in the end, it is the updraft of the joy of just being alive that carries us aloft and puts wind to our sails.

There are two types of effort: physical and mental. Effort transforms those who are lazy. This means we finish what we start. If we start things with great excitement, but then tire and quit, we don't have effort. Completing the job indicates effort.

We are quite diligent when it comes to earning a living. For example, we might get up every morning to bathe and brush our teeth, go to work, and come back home at the end of the day. Usually, we don't skip these routines of work, career, or social activities, and we do that how many times in a day? Somehow, though, our daily application of the Six Principles is easy to avoid. We seem to find endless excuses. In our waking moments, each of us has more enthusiasm or energy to put focus, effort, and time toward ordinary activities rather than towards the Six Principles. There is nothing wrong with that; nevertheless, it is a habitual pattern that we must eventually break to succeed on the path of the Six Principles of enlightened living. We put so much effort toward external things, conventional social values, and principles, but when we think about how much time and energy we spend for inner development, it's not very much time at all.

Worldly cultivation is necessary; cultivating money, cultivating security, is necessary for temporal reasons. When we forget our inner cultivation, when we are busy and so dominated by the sense of external or worldly cultivations, we end up not finding what we are truly seeking: liberation from these same restraints that hold our true potential captive. There is nothing wrong in cultivating worldly things. There is no sin in it. In fact, if we are able to combine the external and internal cultivation together with helping others, we will have a very pure practice of the Six Principles of enlightened living. Moreover, when we listen to enlightened teachers, they talk about the importance of bringing together the two cultivations to see that the two things are not contradictory to each other. When we hold this to be true, we change the quality of our lives. Therefore, there is nothing wrong with worldly cultivation. Worldly cultivation can be very good. If we have successful worldly cultivation, it can support our inner cultivation.

The Six Principles of enlightened living are an inner cultivation, where we develop and reveal their inherent aspects. These aspects are in each and every one of us. They aren't divine qualities in the sense that divine qualities and human qualities are two separate things. The Six Principles are human qualities. They are earthly qualities. Innately, our nature is endowed with the Six Principles of enlightened living. All living things are perfect from the very beginning of their existence, meaning that we innately have all the qualities of omniscience and wisdom. We only have to awaken the divinity that is already within us.

Love, compassion and all the uplifting qualities we aspire to are innately in each of us in the form of an endowment, or seed. Imagine that there is a seed underground, and in order to grow that seed, we have to put a little effort to water it, give it sunlight, and the right kind of nutrients, in order for the seed to grow. The same is true with our innate qualities: our nature is the seed of our potential. To manifest this potential requires work, practice, and training. We can see that the Six Principles are inherent qualities, and they are disciplines we can practice. When we begin to practice generosity, we begin to unfold our inherent generosity. When we practice meditation, we begin to unfold our inherent meditative action. They are already a part of us, otherwise, we wouldn't be able to understand and them as principles. When we practice wisdom, we begin to unfold our inherent wisdom, because it is already there. Whatever we practice of the Six Principles will bring up those inherent qualities. Therefore, this is the ultimate inner cultivation of the intrinsic essence of the Six Principles of enlightened living.

Chapter 8

Just Being is Meditation

The Fifth Principle is meditation, absorption, concentration, and contemplation. Externally it shows up as presence, or connectedness, meditation, and contemplation. Meditation has no other purpose than to bring the mind into an aware state by clearing from it the obstacles created by habit, beliefs, and conditioning, which manifest our attachments and aversions. Meditation is the process of self-cultivation. Internally, it is wise to be focused, centered, aware, and see what is going on, rather than being heedless, mindless, absent-minded, and distracted. It means to see what is going on right here and now. We can do this with a little attention and focus. Inherently, we are always complete. We can never be anything else. Therefore, we mustn't feel lost and look at everyone else who feels lost. You have never been lost. Inherently, you have total presence, although it's something we waste. We overlook it, we deflect it with many defensive shields of distracted, pointless activities. We feel like we only operate on one or two cylinders, and we use the other cylinders to hold back the expression of all that we can be.

In reality, all cylinders are going all the time. How can we not meditate on, contemplate, and reflect upon our lives? Whether doing sitting, standing, or walking meditation, chanting, visualization, yoga, martial arts, breathing exercises, prayers, cooking, painting, writing, or playing a musical instrument in a totally immersed and fully aware manner, the joy of meditation rewards us deeply, and provides us with answers. Meditation is the psychophysical approach to mental cultivation, training, and purification so that our minds can shine and break up the fundamental poison of ignorance at all times. No one can attain wisdom without developing the mind through some form of meditation. Meditation transforms those who are scattered and confused. It centers us in the present moment.

Meditation is the experiential means by which we understand the nature of the inexpressible. Experiencing the exact moment of now in meditation is the dissolution of the duality of 'I and Thou'. It is the realization of the interdependence of all things. In this moment, we realize that nothing can exist without everything else. We can realize *"the selflessness and limitlessness of all existence and with this special insight one can achieve infinite compassion and wisdom."*[9]

---

[9] Transformation of Suffering. A Handbook for Practitioners. By Khenchen Könchog Gyaltshen Rinpoche. Vajra Publications 1996

Chapter 9

Being without the 'I and Thou'

The Sixth Principle is transcendent wisdom. It is indescribable in words. When you get it, you get it. It is pure awareness: a silence resounding like thunder. It is the stillness within. It is truly ineffable, inconceivable, beyond the mind in that it is mind; and yet, it is palpable, and demonstrable in our experience of it, destroying the delusions of the mind. It is our experience. That is the Sixth Principle of enlightened living; it is the embodiment and enactment and can never truly be the intellectual knowledge of something. This is self-realization, the enacting of this knowledge, and the embodying of truth. It is wisdom in action as love, compassion, and excellence. An enlightened life doesn't disparage worldly wisdom of any kind. We acquire knowledge by learning and logical thinking for the sake of serving and helping others. The best form of enlightened living is 'in-lighting' others from darkness to light. We acquire this superior kind of wisdom and knowledge by meditating and contemplating, This way we realize the instinctive truths that are only available in the present moment, the moment of now. It is the wisdom beyond words, and it leads to the purification of our thought processes. Wisdom is an important principle. It is the only principle that can eradicate all distorted and false thinking. It is the mastery of the other five principles of enlightened living, and it is therefore enlightened being.

Chapter 10

Imparting to Others without Ego

Enlightened living is the egoless, skillful imparting to others. This refers to temporal teachings that are clever, expedient devices, not restrained by any fixed standards, they are 'expedient'. In imparting to others, we have to accommodate different kinds of doors of perception.

A method according to the event
A method according to the time
A method according to the circumstances

Because different situations arise, we have to use methods suited to a particular time and place. The methods for skillful imparting aren't constant and unchanging but are impromptu ways for specific reasons. Through these methods, we can persuasively bring others to maturity of understanding. Wisdom transforms those who are ignorant. The bright light disperses the darkness of ignorance. With this principle, we no longer contend or fight. People fight because they lack genuine wisdom and do it to support their ego. If one has true wisdom, one will not fight or struggle. Meditation can help individuals pay attention and be aware of what they can and can't control in the world. Meditation can change our perspective on the things that we are powerless against in daily life. A meditative approach to work can create a cooperative and supportive workplace.

The other five principles: generosity, integrity, patience, diligence, and meditation, are foundations that support the training of enlightened wisdom. Experiential enlightened wisdom is like the general, the chief, or the leader in the battle or war zone. Your ego and its dualistic concepts are like the enemy, the ugly enemy. The five principles are like the armies, the soldiers who actually support or help the chief defeat the enemy. This is a useful analogy to remember. The essence of this training, the Six

Principles, is transcendent enlightened wisdom. The other five principles are like supporters or the founders of the 'in-lighting' wisdom. The Six Principles aren't abstract, religious ideas, concepts, or conduct. Rather they are universal, timeless, ways of conduct, perception, and compassionate wisdom that we can apply in everyday life, no matter where we are: whether home alone or in a very ordinary environment like a traffic jam or in the office. We can practice the Six Principles anytime, anywhere, because it is timeless wisdom.

It seems that when we get to the heart or essence of these enlightened principles, there is less duality of culture, less of the duality of 'I and Thou'. It seems that true teachings, heart-felt teachings, can always mingle with our daily lives. No matter our cultural background, if we look at the Six Principles objectively, they seem so far away from us. However, when we reflect carefully, we will find that the Six Principles are actually a part of us. They are our intrinsic, fundamental qualities that each of us has: Generosity, Patience, Integrity, Effort, and

Meditation. These are very basic enlightened properties in each of us. They are inherent in all us even at birth.

At this point, I would like to stress that each principle completely holds the qualities of the other five. For example, by thoroughly practicing generosity, we can't help but practice the other principles to fully unfold the generosity innate within us. When we practice generosity, are we without integrity? Generosity cannot be practiced without it. When we practice generosity, are we without patience? Generosity cannot be practiced without it. Because our self-cherishing is ever tempting, generosity cannot be practiced without effort. How can we practice generosity without meditating on and contemplating it? In turn, the experience of the practice of generosity awakens us to patience, integrity, effort, and finally awakens us to our innate wisdom.

Generating a little bit of generosity has tremendous benefits: the world becomes a kinder, gentler place. If you fully generate generosity in your being, then you become a Buddha, a fully Awakened One. However, even a small amount will be of great value to the world and to ourselves. Generosity is like the sun dispelling the darkness of night. When generosity arises in your mind, the darkness of ignorance and mental afflictions disappear.

This time is a time of spiritual decline. It is a time where there is an increase in all bad things and a decrease in all good things. The bad things are those that harm all living things. We see this every day in man-made environmental degradation, wars, and corruption, the root of which is the ignorance of self-cherishing at the expense of others. There is an increase in the impulse of sentient beings[10] to harm each other; thinking that by harming others, they will gain some benefit. When sentient beings feel harm or are threatened, they tend to strike out and

---

[10] I use the term of 'sentient beings' here because it accurately describes all living things as sentient, or conscious. It is a term well known in Buddhism and Hinduism.

harm someone else. This shows how the times have declined because through harming others, we harm ourselves and truly do not benefit from such action. In this degenerate age, it is of vital importance to focus on generosity. This is the light in the darkness. This is the cure for the ills of the world. This is what transforms all of these problems and brings about the welfare of all beings.

The practice of the Six Principles of Enlightened Living involves developing these qualities of generosity, integrity, patience, effort, meditation, and transcendent wisdom, which we have, but are dormant, or only potential. The Six Principles are only our potential to most of us. The purpose of practicing the Six Principles and my reminding you and me, on these pages, is to bring this potential, these dormant qualities, to fruition, blossoming into a way of life. We can learn to manifest and unfold these enlightened potentials for the betterment of the world and the beings that live here.

Chapter 11

True Self-Improvement

Now, the Six Principles are like and enlightened seed, or potentiality in our consciousness. Our minds are obscured by selfishness, ignorance, and delusion. They are very powerful hindrances to unfolding our enlightened potential. Training in the Six Principles involves developing, cultivating, and unfolding these enlightened potentials into a state of fruition that manifest in and from direct experience. Therefore, this training involves our internal development. It is not an abstraction. The Six Principles are about developing our inner qualities. This is true self-improvement. To have completion, where completion means wisdom, freedom, love, and compassion. First, we have to go through the process of purification. That means transforming all our limiting habitual tendencies, even transforming knowledge, purifying and transforming our concepts of the world and ourselves. Concepts can be a great hindrance to directly experiencing the natural way of things: their beingness. **The object is to let go and let be.** In order to realize the nature of reality, one has to purify our habitual tendencies, the gross ones, which are easy to point out, and also the subtle ones, which are not so easy to see. They are our concepts, our concepts about who we are in relation to our world. We have to bring them out of the darkness of ignorant self-cherishing. We have to 'in-lighten' all of them. That is why the sixth principle is called enlightened, or transcendent wisdom. Transcending everything, every level of conceptual thought, whether they are holy or unholy, virtuous or non-virtuous, it doesn't matter, we have to transcend every type of concept in order to experience the state of being that is in the present moment. This way, we come to understand that this whole training on the Six Principles is not about acquiring or accumulating more knowledge, but rather about purifying and eradicating everything we invested in our self-cherishing behaviors in this life.

Conclusion

Since each of the Principles of Enlightened Living is an enlightened principle, the wisdom in each one encompasses the other five. For example, if you practice patience towards others and yourself, you will find that you are automatically practicing the other principles. One principle is not separate from the other five. Instead, they are mutually non-exclusive. It is an organic process.

As we wind through the external, internal, and innate aspects of life, we will find the seeds of the Six Principles already within us. We cultivate them outwardly and inwardly and discover that we are already involved in their use. However, it is our way of seeing them that makes us feel far from them and also inadequate in our understanding and practice of them. Even though we are all perfect in the Essence of All That Is, somehow we don't feel perfect enough, never truly satisfied. This is a habit, a distorted way of perceiving, which enlightened vision can correct.

These are the Three Trainings and the Six Principles of Enlightened Living. See what you can find for yourself. Try these in your own life. This is the way to train in them, this is the way to embody and live them, and in which you are already participating.

It might be edifying, empowering, and very gratifying to see that we already participate in the Practice of the Six Principles. The Six Principles are about effortless integration, not restriction. It's about total freedom. It is about fearless and joyous conviction. It is about enhancing meditative awareness by taking it into daily life, and with that effortless and selfless sharing. It is about walking our talk. If it moves and inspires us, we can find teaching tales and books about any and all of the Six Principles in many cultures. The Six Principles have many names, but their essence is the same.

An enlightened life doesn't imply the need for anything in particular. The expression of enlightenment is enlightened activity. Let's manifest that for the benefit of all. That's the meaning of true enlightenment in my opinion. Each of these Six Principles of Enlightened Living is a virtue. We don't have to make it seem like an unattainable fantasy, a heavy trip steeped in catchy phrase-words and sound bites. It doesn't have to be about finding 'the truth'. It can be as simple as being honest, straightforward, and forgiving. To be straightforward and genuine is an extremely profound way to live. That's truth. Just to be ourselves, wholly, through and through, to be genuine, and allow others to be themselves as they are. That is love, acceptance, and the meaning of not harming and the meaning of forgiveness. Forget high-minded notions. A little goodness and warmth go a long way every day.

These principles are principles of enlightened, impeccable living. They are the ways we become enlightened beings and the ways to bring out the best in others and empower others to engender leadership rather than 'followership.' Let us enlighten our world and give birth to leaders rather than just creating more followers. Let us be humble beacons in the world and light the way. We can never receive what we have not given. Let's share our light with the world. Let us awaken our 'in-light' by sharing and enlightening. Giving perfect love enables us to receive perfect love.

You are the light of life as long as you live. 'In-lighten' your life and enlighten the world. Thank you for the opportunity to serve you and for this awakening we have shared. Once again, I bow to the Divine in you. Namaste!

> *I am so grateful.*
> *Seeing that although,*
> *I have difficult times,*
> *Others have it much worse.*
> *I pray for them,*
> *May they see the transitory*
> *Nature of things.*

www.ingramcontent.com/pod-product-compliance
Lightning Source LLC
Chambersburg PA
CBHW051709040426
42446CB00008B/787